G000136558

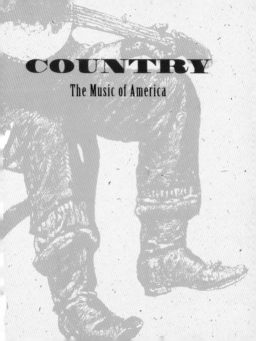

COUNTRY

The Music of America

COUNTRY

THE MUSIC OF AMERICA

Edited by Julie Mars

ARIEL BOOKS

ANDREWS AND McMEEL
KANSAS CITY

With the exception of publicity photographs on pages 17, 28, and 30, all photographs courtesy of the Star File Photo Agency and their photographers: Chuck Pulin, Jeffrey Mayer, Anastasia Pantsios, Vinnie Zuffante, John Lee, David Seelig, Todd Kaplan, Brett Lee, and Larry Kaplan.

ISBN: 0-8362-3113-9

Library of Congress Catalog Card Number: 94-74181

CONTENTS

INTRODUCTION

A woman soulfully recounts a sad story of betrayal and divorce. A man with a deep bass voice laments his lengthy prison term. Together, they bemoan their terrible loneliness and cry about their irreparably broken hearts . . . while around the world, millions of other folks kick back, turn up the volume, and enjoy it.

This is the amazing world of country music. Arguably the most popular form of entertainment on the planet, country cuts across national boundaries to deliver a musical punch that soothes as often as it surprises. From its headquarters in Music City, USA— also known as Nashville, Tennessee—it has spread like country wildfire, igniting its fans to get up and dance, to sing along, and perhaps, at times, to shed a melancholy tear or two. In its relatively short history, its performers have become legends, and record sales have created a whole new interpretation of the phrase "off the charts."

This is the world of train whistles in open spaces, rebel yells and yodels, intricate finger picking, and the confident twang of the pedal steel guitar. From the storefront churches where early musicians were weaned on devotional music to southern juke joints and Texas honky-tonks, country music has blazed a trail out of the heartland of America and captured the heart of the world.

Welcome to country!

THE ROOTS OF COUNTRY

While country music has now spread around the globe, it could only have been born in America. The music's roots lie in the blending of several cultures, but country grew as if it were specifically meant to express the ideas and the identity of the rural American people.

One of these powerful influences was the musical tradition of the Anglo-Celtic immigrants who came from England, Scotland, and Ireland to the South. These hardy people kept their folk songs and musical traditions alive through generation after generation, creating the solid foundation upon which country music is built. African-Americans then contributed complex rhythmic structures and vocal styles. Equally important were the influences of church music, the traveling minstrel theaters, and the popular "medicine shows" that provided entertainment while selling various forms of cure-all "snake tonics." These traveling entertainers spread the music far and wide. It had evolved into a clearly recognizable popular form by the 1920s, considered to be the formal beginning of country music.

The reason its birth is attributed to the 1920s can be summed up in one word: radio. Stations suddenly sprang up throughout the South. Each required live music, and country entertainers were ready to supply it. The broadcasting range was limited to the nearby locality until the "X-stations"—stations using the call letter X, located just across the Mexican border, where there were no regulations on wattage—began to broadcast at wattage three times higher than that permitted in the United States. Suddenly people as far away as Canada could hear so-called "hillbilly music," and the more they heard, the more they wanted.

In 1925, Nashville station WSM began a weekly program called the "WSM Barn Dance." Two years later it was renamed the "Grand Ole Opry." The Opry has continued to thrive ever since.

As country music's popularity grew, many performers hit the road, bringing "tent shows" to every corner of the South, from Virginia to Texas. Thousands of fans attended the shows, and the entertainers, especially the "King of Country Music," Roy Acuff, became legends. Roy Acuff is equally famous inside the business as a founding partner of the Acuff-Rose publishing company, one of the best of its kind, which both paid and protected the songwriters of country music.

The 1930s also brought a new twist to country music—singing cowboys. Intoxicated with the image of the ruggedly individualistic loner in wide-open spaces and the music he created, the budding film industry produced movie after movie starring the beloved Gene Autry and, later, Roy Rogers. These entertainers helped put the "western" in country and western, though soon other western sounds—like the amplified honky-tonk music of east Texas and fully orchestrated western swing

—were incorporated into the overall country music phenomenon.

The country side of country and western expanded too, particularly via bluegrass music. Thanks to innovations in style and the feel-good quality of the music itself, country music was able to thrive in an America deep in the grips of the Great Depression.

The war and post-World War II years were a period of enormous growth for country. The music itself became national (rather than regional), and then international as soldiers carried it all over the world. Six hundred and fifty radio stations broadcast country, record and publishing companies flourished, and the "Camel

Caravans" of Opry stars took to the road to visit military bases far and wide. Ernest Tubb and Hank Williams took over the airwaves, and Kitty Wells hit *Billboard*'s number one spot—the first woman ever to do so. The '50s and '60s brought rock and roll to the forefront, but country never lost its following. It slowly evolved and split into country pop, the "Nashville Sound," rockabilly, and country rock.

Some musical purists regret the path that country has followed. They feel the essential nature of the music changed as it became progressively more commercial and the performers began to use super-stardom rather than authenticity as a measure of success. But change is natural in any vital, evolving art form. There are both innovators and traditionalists in country music, but they all share the same roots, and the music still expresses the spirit of the heartland.

The musicians continue to cut to the core of daily experience to find new melodies, rhythms, and words to uplift the fans. And the fans still show the same respect for the talent and abilities of the musicians as they did when Uncle Dave Macon sang or Uncle Jimmy Thompson played his fiddle.

Country music has always been the music of the folks—and, like the folks, it's here to stay!

THE PIONEERS OF COUNTRY

The Carter Family

When Alvin Pleasant Carter, known as A. P., fell in love with and married Sara Dougherty in 1915, it was a major under-statement to say they made beautiful music together. Joined by Maybelle Addington Carter (A.P.'s sister-in-law), this trio, based in Maces Springs, Virginia, began a legacy of traditional country music that endures even today.

Discovered by the legendary Ralph Peer, the Carter Family first recorded in 1927. Their pure country style, with Maybelle playing the guitar and Sara leading the trio of voices, remained unaffected by any and all commercial trends during the following sixteen years. They recorded material in several styles—blues, spirituals, railroad songs, ballads—but their original sound didn't change—except to get better.

As a major influence on the sound of

country and bluegrass music, the Carters
inspired many other artists to record their
great hits, like "Wabash Cannonball,"
"Single Girl," and "Lonesome Valley."

A.P. died in 1960, just before the
great resurgence of interest in country
music, and Sara retired to California, but
Maybelle remained active in the Nashville
music scene for thirty years after the
Carter Family broke up in 1943.

Jimmie Rodgers

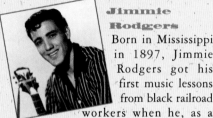

Born in Mississippi in 1897, Jimmie Rodgers got his first music lessons from black railroad workers when he, as a child, was employed as their water boy. His work with the railroad continued for almost fourteen years until ill health forced him to quit. Then he turned to music, and soon thereafter Jimmie, like the Carter Family, was discovered by Ralph Peer. Peer, in fact, recorded Jimmie (billed as the "Singing Brakeman") and the Carters in the same week in 1927.

From that point on, it was a classic success story. Within half a year, Rodgers was a rich man—earning, in the late 1920s, a phenomenal $2,000 a month. In the six years that followed, he recorded more than 110 songs, combining his country-style crooning with the "blue yodel" for which he soon became famous.

Rodgers was known for his musical innovations. He sang to the Hawaiian-style accompaniments of steel guitar and ukulele, used jazz-flavored arrangements, and sometimes imitated a train whistle as he sang. He enjoyed great popularity, and his renditions of such songs as "Train Whistle Blues," "T for Texas," "Daddy and Home," and "TB Blues," are considered classic.

Unfortunately, Rodgers died of tuberculosis in 1933 in New York City. He had completed twelve new recordings the day before he died, although he was so sick that a cot had to be set up in the studio. Jimmie Rodgers's body was carried home by train as songwriters around the country composed a flood of tribute songs.

Roy Acuff

Roy Acuff thought he would have a career in sports, but a bad case of sunstroke while he was at a Florida training camp for the New York Yankees shattered that dream for good. Bedridden afterward for over a year, Acuff amused himself by learning to play his father's fiddle. A local doctor who was about to hit the road with his medicine show overheard Roy and invited him along. No one could have guessed that the shy young fiddler would become the undisputed "King of Country

Music" and the first living person elected to the Country Music Hall of Fame.

Acuff started on the radio in Knoxville in 1933, began recording in 1936, and finally made it to the Grand Ole Opry, after repeated attempts, in 1938. Favorable audience response secured him a permanent Opry spot, though at the time it was almost unheard of for the Opry to hire a singer as a headliner. From there it was a quick jump to national celebrity.

In 1940, Roy played himself in the first of seven Hollywood movies about the Grand Ole Opry. All this, plus the huge success of the publishing company he founded in 1942, Acuff-Rose Publications, and his candidacy for the governorship of Tennessee in 1948, proves that Roy Acuff had the stuff of which legends are made. In fact, he was so beloved in country circles that he lived out his final days in a home built on the grounds of Opryland.

He will always be remembered for such tunes as "The Great Speckled Bird," "Just to Ease My Worried Mind," and "Precious Jewel."

COUNTRY: THE MUSIC OF AMERICA

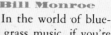

Bill Monroe

In the world of blue-grass music, if you're looking for the source, you need look no further than Bill Monroe. Starting out as one of the "Monroe Brothers" and continuing with his own band, the "Bluegrass Boys," Bill, with his mandolin, almost single-handedly carved a well-respected niche for this beloved type of music.

Bill Monroe's original break came in 1936 when a talent scout for Victor

Records heard the Monroe Brothers play in North Carolina and set up a recording session. This resulted in a best-selling single, "What Would You Give Me in Exchange," followed by more recording sessions and radio work. The Brothers separated in 1938, but Bill's group, the "Bluegrass Boys," earned a spot on the Grand Ole Opry in 1939—and stayed for decades.

Still grateful for his tremendous success as both a performer and a source of traditional music values and sounds, Bill Monroe is renowned for giving encouragement and help to other musicians.

Hank Williams

Hank Williams is often called the greatest figure in country music, so it's no surprise that his music and popularity have outlived him. But it can also be said that Hank was the first crossover artist. Although his music was firmly rooted in country traditions, it ultimately transcended those borders to become popular music as well.

Hank's roots are similar to those of many country artists. His mother played

the organ at the local church, and his formal training came from a local black
bluesman, "Tee Tot" Rufe Payne, who
taught him the rudiments of blues with a
jazz and pop twist. Later, he shaped his
sound in the local Alabama honky-tonks.
His personal life was as tragic as some of
the songs he sang: he died in 1952, at the
age of twenty-eight, of alcohol-related
heart disease.

Hank's talent was enormous, and his
sincerity clearly showed through his music.
That, coupled with the guidance of
Fred and Wesley Rose of Acuff-Rose
Publications, put him over the top, and
into the hearts of millions of fans worldwide.
He will always be remembered for his

"Lovesick Blues," "Your Cheatin' Heart," "I'm So Lonesome I Could Cry," "Hey Good-Lookin'," "Jambalaya," and scores of others, and his place of honor as one of the great forces in American culture is secure.

Kitty Wells

Kitty Wells, the "Queen of Country Music," was born Muriel Deason in Nashville. She was originally a singer with a band called "The Tennessee Mountain Boys," but her career finally took off when she went solo. In 1952, Kitty hit the number one spot on the charts with "It Wasn't God Who Made Honky-Tonk Angels." She was the first female performer to chalk up that honor, and her later recordings consistently made the Top Ten. Beloved as she is for such hits as "A Wedding Ring Ago" and "Whose Shoulder Will You Cry On," Kitty Wells is also deeply respected for her groundbreaking role in introducing women to the inner circle of country music success.

Patsy Cline

Patsy Cline, otherwise known as Virginia Patterson Hensley, had struggled in the music business for several years before her rendition of "Walkin' After Midnight" on the Arthur Godfrey Talent Scout Show in 1957 took first prize. Fan reaction guaranteed that she would never struggle professionally again. Her recordings of such classics as "I Fall to Pieces," "Sweet Dreams," and "Crazy" assured her a place on the pop as well as the country charts and ushered in

the modern age of women singers in
country music. The whole country music
community—and the world—deeply
mourned her early and tragic death in an
airplane crash on March 5, 1963.

Johnny Cash

Johnny Cash was born
to a family of southern
farmers who share-
cropped during the
Great Depression.
Along with his
parents, who pro-
vided his early
musical education, the
battery-operated radio that brought

music from faraway cities exerted a major formative influence and ultimately led to his eclectic style.

After military service, Cash settled in Memphis and formed the "Tennessee Three." Although they played locally, Sam Phillips eventually signed them on, and they became one of the foremost groups on the Sun Records roster, which included Elvis Presley, Roy Orbison, and Carl Perkins. Collectively, the sound was called rockabilly—a lively mixture of country and rock and roll.

Cash's eclectic taste resulted in many styles of music from rockabilly to folk, from devotional to western. Famous for his outlaw image and such tunes as

"Folsom Prison Blues," "A Boy Named Sue," "The Man in Black," and "Pickin' Time," Johnny Cash is universally considered one of the country music greats.

Loretta Lynn

The title "Coal Miner's Daughter" sums up Loretta's life and career: her roots were pure, traditional country. Born in Butcher's Holler, Kentucky, she was raised in the hardscrabble southern rural fashion in which a woman's place was in the home. But apparently that didn't sit quite right with Loretta, because she would become the major artist of the 1960s and 1970s to establish women as independent stars. With the expert assistance of her husband, Mooney, and others who recognized and supported her talent, Loretta was able to remain true to her traditional roots as she expressed the aspirations of most modern women—a readiness to stake out an equal position to that of men. Songs like "Don't Come Home a'Drinkin' with Lovin' on Your Mind," "Your Squaw Is on the Warpath," and "The Pill" speak for themselves.

Tammy Wynette

Born on a cotton farm in Mississippi, Virginia Wynette Pugh grew up fantasizing about being a singer. It took one divorce and a risky move to Nashville in 1966 for her to make it a reality. She signed with Epic Records and made several highly respected singles before she soared over the top with "Stand by Your Man" in 1968. This single sold more copies than any other recording by a solo female and established Tammy Wynette as a country superstar. She married and divorced three times—the great George Jones was her husband for a while—which may have inspired another record that will always be associated with Tammy: "D-I-V-O-R-C-E." With her winning personality and superb voice, Tammy gracefully stands at the forefront of women in country music.

Dolly Parton

Dolly Parton is a classic success story. Despite her difficult background as one of twelve children, Dolly was born to sing—and she knew it. By the age of ten she was already appearing on Knoxville TV, so it was inevitable that she would go to Nashville directly after high school graduation in 1964. What was not so predictable was her enormous success.

She was signed immediately by Monument Records. In 1967, her hit "Dumb Blonde" secured her a featured role on the "Porter Wagoner Show." After she went solo in '74, her successes piled up: Country Music Association's Female Vocalist of the Year in 1975 and '76, her own syndicated TV show, and parts in Hollywood movies. Her unforgettable hits include "Coat of Many Colors," "In the Good Old Days (When Times Were Bad)," and "Just Because I'm a Woman."

By 1983, she was the top earner in Las Vegas entertainment at $350,000 per week—more than Frank Sinatra or Diana Ross. Dolly's famous physical beauty, her expert showmanship, and above all her extraordinary performance and songwriting talents, have made her into country's best known female legend.

Ricky Skaggs

Ricky Skaggs is known in the business as the man who took the "pop" out of country and returned country to its roots. As a bluegrass-influenced player interested in traditional music, Ricky remained loyal to the acoustic sound even in the late 1970s and early 1980s, when it was not popular. His persistence resulted in "Uncle Pen," the first solo bluegrass tune to hit the number one spot in forty years.

Ricky Skaggs is deeply respected in the music community for his high harmony and virtuoso instrumentation, and he continues to demonstrate that folks just plain *like* basic country music.

Randy Travis

A country boy from Marshville, North Carolina, Randy Travis got off to a slow start as a part-time singer/short order cook in Nashville before he blasted off— straight to the top of the charts in 1985.

With three number one hits in rapid succession—"1982," "On the Other Hand," and "Diggin' Up the Bones"—this quiet, unassuming man, who hadn't yet hit thirty years old, received critical and popular acclaim for his debut album, *Storms of Life,* and followed a grueling schedule of personal appearances that cemented his place in the hearts of country music fans.

Randy was elected the Country Music Association's Best Male Vocalist two times running. His low-key style and down-home country music roots are totally appealing, and his rise to fame has been nothing less than meteoric in recent country music history.

GREAT COUNTRY
SONG TITLES

Somehow, just a song title is enough to
evoke the essence of country. Here are
some remarkable titles, and the recording
artists who first put them in the groove.

COUNTRY: THE MUSIC OF AMERICA

**DADDY WAS A PREACHER BUT MAMA
WAS A GO-GO GIRL**
(Joanne Neel)

DIVORCE ME C.O.D.
(Merle Travis)

**DON'T COME HOME A'DRINKIN' WITH
LOVIN' ON YOUR MIND**
(Loretta Lynn)

**IF I SAID YOU HAD A BEAUTIFUL BODY,
WOULD YOU HOLD IT AGAINST ME?**
(Bellamy Brothers)

COUNTRY: THE MUSIC OF AMERICA

I'M JUST HERE TO GET MY BABY OUT OF JAIL
(Karl Davis & Harty Taylor)

THE INTERSTATE IS COMING THROUGH MY OUTHOUSE
(Billy Edd Wheeler)

IN THE GOOD OLD DAYS WHEN TIMES WERE BAD
(Dolly Parton)

I WAS COUNTRY WHEN COUNTRY WASN'T COOL
(Barbara Mandrell)

COUNTRY: THE MUSIC OF AMERICA

PICK ME UP ON YOUR WAY DOWN
(Charlie Walker)

REDNECKS, WHITE SOCKS, AND BLUE RIBBON BEER
(Johnny Russell)

SO ROUND, SO FIRM, SO FULLY PACKED
(Merle Travis)

TAKE THIS JOB AND SHOVE IT
(Johnny Paycheck)

WHO WANTS A SLIGHTLY USED WOMAN?
(Connie Cato)

COUNTRY: THE MUSIC OF AMERICA

YOU CAN'T ROLLER SKATE IN A BUFFALO HERD
(Roger Miller)

YOU'RE THE HANGNAIL IN MY LIFE
(Hoyt Axton)

YOUR TEARS ARE JUST INTEREST ON THE LOAN
(Don Reno & Red Smiley)

TRAVELIN', CHEATIN', AND DRINKIN'...

TRAVELIN'...

Ride a horse, take a train, or drive a truck, but stay on the move! The belief that a person has to keep on going and never settle down (even if the loneliness leads to a serious case of the blues) is basic

49

to the rhythms of the music . . . and it shows in the song titles. Here are just a few of the traveling songs that keep fans on the country music road.

CONVOY
(C. W. McCall)

FREIGHT TRAIN BOOGIE
(the Delmore Brothers)

HOBO BILL'S LAST RIDE
(Jimmie Rodgers)

I'VE RANGED, I'VE ROAMED, AND I'VE TRAVELED
(Jimmie Rodgers)

COUNTRY: THE MUSIC OF AMERICA

LONESOME ROAD BLUES
(Henry Whitter)

LOST HIGHWAY
(Hank Williams)

RAILROAD BLUES
(Kirk and Sam McGee)

TRAVELING BLUES
(Jimmie Rodgers)

TRUCK DRIVER'S BLUES
(Cliff Bruner)

WABASH CANNONBALL
(A. P. Carter)

CHEATIN'...

Broken hearts, lovers left behind, and marriage—to the wrong person. They all lead to—or result from—cheatin' . . . and cheatin' is a tradition in country music, as these song titles prove.

BACK STREET AFFAIR
(Webb Pierce)

FOOLIN' AROUND
(Buck Owens)

I KNOW YOU'RE MARRIED BUT I LOVE YOU STILL
(Red Smiley and Don Reno)

COUNTRY: THE MUSIC OF AMERICA

ONE HAS MY NAME, the OTHER HAS MY HEART
(Jimmy Wakely)

PAYING FOR THAT BACK STREET AFFAIR
(Kitty Wells)

SECRET LOVE
(Otis "Slim" Whitman)

TRYING TO LOVE TWO WOMEN
(Oak Ridge Boys)

YOUR CHEATIN' HEART
(Hank Williams)

DRINKIN'...

Drinkin' always leads to trouble in country music, but it also leads to great songs. Here are just a few of the serious drinking songs that are country standards.

THE BOTTLE LET ME DOWN
(Merle Haggard)

BUBBLES IN MY BEER
(Cindy Walker)

DON'T SELL DADDY ANYMORE WHISKEY
(Molly O'Day)

COUNTRY: THE MUSIC OF AMERICA

DRINKING THING
(Gary Stewart)

THE DRUNKARD'S CHILD
(Jimmie Rodgers)

GAMBLING BARROOM BLUES
(Jimmie Rodgers)

HANGOVER BLUES
(The Maddox Brothers and Rose)

COUNTRY: THE MUSIC OF AMERICA

IF DRINKIN' DON'T KILL ME HER MEMORY WILL
(George Jones)

WHISKEY BENT AND HELL BOUND
(Hank Williams, Jr.)

WHITE LIGHTNING
(George Jones)

COUNTRY QUOTES

"Hillbilly gets to be country when you can afford one of these."

Minnie Pearl, while petting her mink stole, after being asked to describe the difference between hillbilly and country music.

"I was in the audience, Johnny."

> *Merle Haggard to Johnny Cash, when Cash didn't remember Haggard's presence at the "Live at San Quentin" show.*

"Yeah, but not enough to hurt my playin'."

> *An unnamed Nashville studio sideman when asked if he could read music.*

"Why shucks, a man don't get warmed up in an hour."

Uncle Jimmy Thompson, an eighty-year-old fiddler, after playing solo for a solid hour on the radio show that would later become the Grand Ole Opry.

"I have to keep her working so I can afford whiskey."

Mooney Lynn, husband of Loretta Lynn, when asked why she continued to work after accomplishing all her goals.

"Hell, it don't much matter where you record, anyway. It's what you put in the groove."

Mérle Haggard, on recording in Nashville.

"The principal appeal of the Opry is a homey one. It sends forth the aroma of bacon and eggs frying on the kitchen stove on a bright spring morning. That aroma is welcomed all the way from Maine to California."

Judge George D. Hay, "the Solemn Old Judge," on the appeal of the Grand Ole Opry.

"We have been married twenty-five years, and I am only going to give her one more week and if she don't square up, she is out of here."

Ken Dudney, after being asked about his marriage to country superstar Barbara Mandrell.

"Why you singin' this music? It ain't gonna get you nowhere."

A comment made to Charley Pride, from his sister.

"Some day I'd like to quit, buy some kind of business, sit down and watch the dog bark at the car while I drink a beer."

Freddy Fender

"Just 'cause I wear a hat ain't got a thing to do with where my head's at."

Billy Joe Shaver

COUNTRY: THE MUSIC OF AMERICA

"You know, I never wrote a tune in my life. All that music's in the air around you all the time. I was just the first one to reach up and pull it out."

Bill Monroe

"A good country song taps into strong undercurrents of family, faith, and patriotism . . . and of course train wrecks, romances turned sour, and cheatin' hearts."

George Bush

"It can be explained in just one word: sincerity. When a hillbilly sings a crazy song, he feels crazy. When he sings, 'I Laid My Mother Away,' he sees her a-laying right there in the coffin. He sings more sincere than most entertainers because the hillbilly was raised tougher than most entertainers. You got to know a lot about hard work. You got to have smelt a lot of mule manure before you can sing like a hillbilly."

Hank Williams, on the success of country music.

LITTLE-KNOWN FACTS

Johnny Cash, the "Man in Black," has a well-developed bad boy image, but in reality he only spent one night in jail in 1966—after he was caught illegally picking flowers.

The great Hank Williams quietly died, presumably of heart failure, in the backseat of a car on the way to give a concert in Ohio in 1953—on the very same day that the powers-that-were in the Grand Ole Opry decided to give him another chance after having fired him. His friends, riding in the front seat, never noticed that Hank had passed on until a policeman who stopped them remarked that the man in the backseat looked dead.

Roy Rogers, TV's Singing Cowboy, had the body of his horse, Trigger, stuffed and placed in the Roy Rogers–Dale Evans Museum in California.

COUNTRY: THE MUSIC OF AMERICA

A Nashville studio sideman can earn up to $200,000 per year.

During World War II, country music was so popular worldwide that Japanese troops included the "King of Country Music" in their battle cries. As they stormed American military lines, Japanese soldiers shouted, "To hell with Roosevelt! To hell with Babe Ruth! To hell with Roy Acuff!"

HARD TIME

Jail terms, the sexy outlaw image, and, perhaps most of all, the inspirational human spirit that would belt out a song from behind bars, have long since been a big part of country music. And while some of the stars have done hard jail

time—Merle Haggard and Freddy
Fender, for example—most of the "bad
boys" are actually pretty nice guys. But
real or not, "jailhouse charm" has resulted
in some great prison songs. Here are just
a few of the titles from this country music
subgenre:

A WEEK IN A COUNTRY JAIL
(Tom T. Hall)

BUSTED
(Johnny Cash)

FOLSOM PRISON BLUES
(Johnny Cash)

COUNTRY: THE MUSIC OF AMERICA

FORT WORTH JAIL
(Tex Ritter)

IN THE JAILHOUSE NOW
(Jimmie Rodgers)

MAXIMUM SECURITY TO MINIMUM WAGE
(Don King)

NINETY DAYS
(Jimmy Dean)

THE OUTLAW'S PRAYER
(Johnny Paycheck)

THERE AIN'T NO GOOD CHAIN GANG
(Waylon Jennings & Johnny Cash)

THE ABCs OF COUNTRY

Blue Yodel: Made famous by the "Singing Brakeman," Jimmie Rodgers, this hallmark of country music combines the vocal sounds of traditional yodeling with the soulful blues inspired by the music of southern blacks.

COUNTRY: THE MUSIC OF AMERICA

Camel Caravan: A group of country music entertainers who traveled to military bases to boost morale during World War II under the sponsorship of the Grand Ole Opry and the R. J. Reynolds Tobacco Company.

Dobro: Originally designed and created by the Dopera Brothers, prior to the age of electronic amplification, the Dobro amplified the volume of guitars via metal discs that vibrated under the strings. The Dobro became common in country music in the 1930s.

COUNTRY: THE MUSIC OF AMERICA

Event Song: A song that exploits the tragic or scandalous news stories of the day, generally ending with a moral lesson.

Grand Ole Opry: It began as a radio show in 1925 and has continued every Saturday night since, setting the standard of country music and showcasing all the greats. Today the Grand Ole Opry is headquartered in Opryland, USA, a four hundred-acre entertainment park in Nashville.

Hillbilly: Originally a term for backwoods, down-home Southern folk, it was first used to describe country music in 1925 and quickly became a catchphrase, though many entertainers resented what they considered the negative connotations of the word.

Juke Joint: A tavern or roadhouse in the South where, in the late '20s and '30s, country music was popularized due to the presence of a jukebox capable of holding twelve records.

King Records: A Cincinnati-based record company that specialized in country, blues, and gospel music in the early 1950s. The personal interest and risk taking on the part of founder Sydney Nathan resulted not in only great country, blues, and boogie, but also in cross-racial recordings.

Nudie Suit: Sequined, fringed, spangled, and highly decorated western costumes designed and created by Nudie the tailor (Nudie Cohen). As country superstars collected Nudie suits, the prices rose from a few hundred to several thousand dollars.

Okeh Records: The record company that launched both "race records" (featuring black singers) and the "white hillbilly" music industry. The force behind Okeh, Ralph Peer, is considered by all to have been a country music visionary.

Pearl, Minnie: Born Sarah Ophelia Colley, Minnie Pearl became a regular on the Grand Ole Opry. She is known for her straw hat (with the price tag showing) and her signature greeting of "How-dee, I'm so proud to be here!"

Quartets: A country music phenomenon in the late 1970s, these background groups that finally stepped into the spotlight included the Oak Ridge Boys and the Statler Brothers.

Rambling Man: Starting with Jimmie Rodgers and continuing until today, this is the romanticized image of the man on the move, alone with his loneliness, his sad thoughts, and his music.

Saga Song: Somewhat similar to the "event song," the saga song told a fictional story, often focusing on mythical American heroes.

Travis Picking: A style of finger picking popularized by Merle Travis. In it, the thumb establishes the bass line while the other fingers formulate the melody on the treble strings.

Ukulele: Introduced to country music along with the steel guitar in the 1920s; its roots are in Hawaii. It was popularized by the traveling Hawaiian musicians who began to tour America after World War I.

COUNTRY: THE MUSIC OF AMERICA

Vaudeville: The entertainment movement credited with creating professional song-writers and spreading their music throughout the South.

X-Stations: Radio stations on the Mexican side of the border with so powerful a broadcasting range that country music filled the airways as far away as Canada, beginning in the 1930s.

Yodeling: Though no one is exactly sure how yodeling worked its way into country music, it can be heard as far back as the 1890s and remains a well-respected tradition today.

Zydeco: A specific type of rural southern music found in and around the Louisiana bayous. Featuring guitar, washboard, and accordion, zydeco combines music of French origin with the blues and elements of Caribbean music.

The text of this book was set in American Garamond, the display was set in Madrone and Birch.

Book Design by
Diane Stevenson/Snap-Haus Graphics